DOUBLE ENTRY BOOKKEEPING

Toye Adelaja

DOUBLE ENTRY BOOKEEPING

Copyright © 2015 by (Toye Adelaja)

TABLE OF CONTENTS

CHAPTER 1

1.0 Double Entry Principle

Double entry principle is the recording of a financial transaction twice in a book of account. The rule states that for every debit entry, there must be a corresponding credit entry, and for every credit entry, there must be a corresponding debit entry. It is the foundation of Financial Accounting. The recording of every financial transaction is based on the principle of double entry.

Without applying the double entry principles in accounting records, the accounting records would only reflect a partial view of an entity's record.

A financial transaction is an event which involves money or payments, such as the act of buying and selling goods and services, depositing money into bank accounts, borrowing money from a lender, and refunding money to the lender.

A financial transaction can also be defined as an agreement or a communication between a seller and a buyer to exchange goods, services or financial instruments. In financial accounting, a financial transaction (an accounting transaction) must be recorded on the books, and the transaction will be recorded differently if the company uses accrual accounting rather than cash accounting.

Accrual accounting records transactions immediately revenues are realized or expenses are incurred, while cash accounting records transactions when the business actually receives or spends money. Accrual accounting is commonly used in financial accounting, and hence it is adopted in this book.

In every financial transaction, two parties must be involved; the party that gives, and the party that receives. In some circumstances, the giver can be the seller or the lender, while the receiver can be the buyer or the borrower. Each party must keep a record of its financial transaction. The record of the financial transaction is kept in the books of accounts.

The accounting books of each party must state (contain) the accounts of a giver and the accounts of a receiver.

1.1 What is bookkeeping?

Bookkeeping is a systematic recording of financial transactions in books of accounts. It will be explained in chapter 5.

Double entry principle must be applied in bookkeeping in order to make it effective.

DIFFERENCES BETWEEN BOOKKEEPING AND ACCOUNTING

Bookkeeping and accounting are two important tools for communicating the financial operations, performances and positions of a business entity to stakeholders of the business.

It is necessary for every organization both profit making entity and non-profit making entity to record and keep books of financial transactions. Accounting is much broader than bookkeeping.

Bookkeeping involves only the record keeping aspect of accounting. It is a systematic recording of daily transactions of a business.

Accounting involves the whole process of recording, classifying, summarizing, reporting, analyzing, interpreting, and communicating of financial performances and positions of a business to stakeholders for decision making.

Bookkeeping is just a component of Accounting. Accounting is a system, while Bookkeeping is just a sectional part of an Accounting system.

1.2 What is double entry bookkeeping?

The principle of double entry book-keeping states that; every financial transaction must be treated twice in a book of accounts. The rule of double entry book-keeping states that: for every debit entry, there must be a corresponding credit entry, and for every credit entry there must be a corresponding debit entry.

When the books of accounts of a business are maintained in accordance with the rule of double entry, the bookkeeping involved is called double entry book-keeping.

The principle of double entry bookkeeping was devised by an Italian called Luca Pacioli in 1494.

Every business owner or business entity must keep a book which contains a double entry for every unique transaction. It means that in the book of a business owner, two accounts must be open for a single transaction. One account must be debited and the other account is credited with the financial transaction involved.

The procedure for double entry bookkeeping are as follows:

1. Identify whether the financial transaction involved is an asset, liability, expense or income.

2. Identify the two accounts to be recorded.

3. Identify the accounts to be debited and the accounts to be credited.

The abbreviation of debit and credit can be denoted by Dr. and Cr. respectively.

1.3 The format below could be used in recording a transaction using double entry principles.

Nature of Accounts	Debit	Credit
Assets	Increase	Decrease
Income	Decrease	Increase
Liabilities	Decrease	Increase
Expenses	Increase	Decrease
Owner's Equity	Decrease	Increase

The following are brief explanations of the format above:

1. When an asset increases, the value should be debited with the increase. When an asset decreases, the amount concerned should be credited.

2. When a liability increases, the value of the increase should be credited. When a liability decreases, the amount concerned should be debited.

3. When income increases, it should be credited with the value of increase. When income decreases, it should be debited with the value of the decrease.

4. When an expense increases, it should be debited with the value of increase. When an expense decreases, it should be credited with the value of the decrease.

ILLUSTRATION 1

Mr. Jones contributed the sum of $5,000 as capital for the new business, placing it with its bank.

You are required to record the above transaction in the book of Mr. Jones.

SOLUTION

Procedures for the double entry bookkeeping are as follows:

1. The financial transaction involves money deposited into a bank to commence business (cash deposited in the bank).

2. The two accounts to be recorded are Bank Accounts, and Capital Accounts.

3. Debit bank accounts because it increase, and credit capital accounts because it increase.

Note:

According to the question, the two accounts should be recorded in the book of Mr. Jones.

Note: The procedures above should not be written in an examination. They are meant for explanations.

In the book of Mr. Jones

Ledger Accounts

Dr.	Bank Accounts		Cr.
	$		$
Capital	5,000		

Dr.	Capital Accounts		Cr.
	$		$
		Bank	5,000

ILLUSTRATION 2

From $5,000 in the Bank Accounts, Mr. Jones paid out $850 to a supplier for the purchase of raw material required in a factory, and paid $1,350 for the acquisition of a motor vehicle. $900 was paid as annual office rent from the bank accounts.

Required: post to the ledger accounts.

SOLUTION:

Rules of double entry should be followed in solving this question.

Ledgers are as follows:

We have to reproduce initial bank accounts and capital accounts before posting the new transaction into the ledger accounts in order to make the illustration 2 clearer.

		Bank Accounts	
	$		$
Bank	5,000	Purchases	850
		Motor Vehicle	1,350
		Rent Expense	900

Capital Accounts			
$		$	
		Bank	5,000

Purchases Accounts			
	$		$
Bank	850		

Motor Vehicle			
	$		$
Bank	1,350		

Rent Expense			
	$		$
Bank	900		

Notes on the above transaction are as follows:

a) Payment of $5,000 into the bank account is the contribution of capital by the proprietor. An amount used in setting up a business is called capital. Assume zero balance in the bank account, the amount in the bank is now increased by the deposit of $5,000 and according to the format 1.3 above, when an asset increases, it should be debited. Assume zero balance on capital account, capital now increases by $5,000. This should be credited according to the format.

b) All goods purchased for resale are called purchases and are recorded in purchases accounts. Purchases account should be debited with the amount of goods purchased ($850) because the purchases (expenditures) increase. Bank accounts will be credited because the bank account has reduced by $850 (the payment of raw materials).

c) Acquisition of motor vehicle will be debited to motor vehicle account because it increases motor vehicle (asset), while the payment for the acquisition by check will be credited to bank account because the payment reduces bank account (asset)

ILLUSTRATION 3

Mr. Andrew, the owner of Andrew enterprise contributes $100,000 on July 1, 2015, to commence a business, by depositing it into Bank account of the business.

Record the above to journal, and ledger.

SOLUTION:

The transaction above involves cash deposited into bank by Mr. Andrew to start a business (Andrew Enterprise)

In the Book of Andrew Enterprises

Journal Entry

		Dr.	Cr.
Date		$	$
July 1, 2015	Bank	100,000	

July 1, 2015   Capital   100,000
Being the value of cash contributed to start a business

Bank Account

2015		$	2015		$
July 1	Capital	100,000			

Capital Account

2015		$	2015		$
			July 1	Bank	100,000

NOTE:

The owner of the business is different from the business. This is the reason why Mr. Andrew is treated as different from his business.

If Mr. Andrew withdraws cash from Andrew enterprise's bank accounts for his personal use, the bank accounts will be credited while the drawings account will be debited.

ILLUSTRATION 4
Assume that Andrew enterprise purchased goods worth $45,000 from TY Ltd., on July 7, 2015.

You are required to enter the transaction in a journal and post to ledgers.

SOLUTION
Steps:

    1) In whose book are you recording the transaction?

2) Identify the transaction involved.
3) Identify the two accounts required to be posted.
4) Identify the account to be debited and the account to be credited.
5) Record your entries.

In the books of Andrew Enterprise

Journal Entry 1

		Dr.	Cr.
2015		$	$
July, 7	Purchases	45,000	
July,7	TY Ltd.		45,000

Being the value of goods purchased

Purchases Accounts

2015		$	
July 7	TY Ltd.	45,000	

TY Ltd.

2015		$	2015		$
July 7			July 7	Purchases	45,000

ILLUSTRATION 5

Assume that Andrew enterprise paid **TY Ltd.** by check on August 15, 2015.

You are required to record the above transaction in a ledger.

In the book of Andrew Enterprise

TY Ltd.

2015		$	2015		$
August 15	Bank	45,000	July 7	Purchases	45,000

Bank Accounts

2015		$	2015		$
July 7	Capital	100,000	August 15	TY Ltd.	45,000

1.4 Cash Transactions

Cash transactions are ones that are settled immediately by cash. Cash transactions also include transaction made through checks.

In accounting, there are two ways to treat cash transactions.

Alternative 1

Where financial transactions such as sales, purchases and expenses involve immediate acceptance or payment of cash, **two transactions may be involved.** One transaction is the existence of a contract and the other transaction is the receipt of money or payment of money. According to the rule of double entry, two entries will be made for each transaction. There will be a total of four entries for the two transactions.

ILLUSTRATION 6

Assume that Andrew enterprise sold goods worth $5,000 to Mrs. Eunice on August 23, 2015, and Mrs. Eunice paid immediately by credit transfer into the bank accounts of Andrew Enterprise.

Record the above transactions in the books of Andrew Enterprise.

Journal Entry 1

Date		Dr. $	Cr. $
August 23, 2015	Mrs. Eunice	5,000	
August 23, 2015	Sales		5,000

Being the value of goods sold to Mrs. Eunice

Journal Entry 2

		Dr. $	Cr. $
August 23, 2015	Bank	5,000	
August 23, 2015	Mrs. Eunice		5,000

Being the value of credit transfer (Bank) by Mrs. Eunice

Mrs. Eunice Accounts

Date 2015		$	Date 2015		$
August 23	Sales	5,000	August 23	Bank	5,000

Sales Accounts

Date 2015	$	Date 2015		$
		August 23	Mrs. Eunice	5,000

Bank Account

2015		$	2015 August		$
July 1	Capital	100,000	15	TY Ltd.	45,000
August 23	Mrs. Eunice	5,000			

Note:

- The recording of $5,000 in 4 times at the same date signifies 4 entries. This is possible when there is a contract of sales, and acceptance of cash at the same time.

- The bank account above is brought down from previous illustration, and the bank transaction in the current illustration is added to it.

Alternative 2

Where financial transactions such as sales, purchases and expenses involve immediate acceptance or payment of cash, one transaction may be involved. The transaction may be an immediate receipt of cash for goods sold or services rendered.

Assume you are given the same information as in illustration 6. You are required to post necessary ledger accounts.

SOLUTION

Sales Accounts

2015		$	2015		$
			Aug. 23	Bank	5,000

Bank Account

2015		$	2015		$
July 1	Capital	100,000	August	TY Ltd.	45,000

Aug. 23	Sales	5,000

Note: The above **alternative 2** is a short and direct method. It is mostly recommended where financial transactions are many.

1.5 Receipt of Cash/Check in a Future Period

The method applied in **alternative 1of** figure 1.4 will also be applied here. The only difference is the date of acceptance of cash.

Illustration 7

Assume that Andrew enterprise sold goods worth $5,000 to Mrs. Eunice on August 23, 2015, and Mrs. Eunice paid for the goods on October 1, 2015, by credit transfer into the bank account of Andrew Enterprise.

Record the above transaction in the book of Andrew Enterprise.

Solution

Journal Entry 1

		Dr.	Cr.
Date		$	$
August 23, 2015	Mrs. Eunice	5,000	
August 23, 2015	Sales		5,000

Being the value of goods sold to Mrs. Eunice

Journal Entry 2

		Dr.	Cr.
		$	$
October 1, 2015	Bank	5,000	
October 1, 2015	Mrs. Eunice		5,000

Being the value of credit transfer (Bank) by Mrs. Eunice

Mrs. Eunice Accounts

Date 2015		$	Date 2015		$
August 23	Sales	5,000	October 1	Bank	5,000

Sales Accounts

Date 2015		$	Date 2015		$
			August 23	Mrs. Eunice	5,000

Bank Accounts

2015		$	2015		$
			August		
July 1	Capital	100,000	15	TY Ltd.	45,000
October 1	Mrs. Eunice	5,000			

1.6 Advantages of Double Entry Bookkeeping

1. It provides a complete record of each transaction.

2. It provides a check on the arithmetical accuracy of the clerical work.

3. It provides an effective control of the business.

4. It facilitates the preparation of financial statements.

1.7 Ledger

A ledger is a principal book of account. It contains all the accounts of a business entity, and is kept on the double entry principles.

Ledger can be sub-divided into the following:

a) Sales Ledger: It contains debtors' accounts or accounts receivable. It can also be referred to as debtors' ledger.

b) Purchases Ledger: It contains creditors' accounts or accounts payable. It can also be referred to as creditors' ledger.

c) General Ledger contains the real and nominal accounts. It can also be referred to as impersonal ledger. It contains income accounts, expenditure accounts, and real asset accounts.

d) Private Ledger contains capital account, and drawings account of the proprietor.

e) Cash book is a ledger. It contains cash and bank accounts. It is also a book of original entry.

1.8 Balancing -off Ledger Accounts

At the end of each accounting period, the total values on the debit side of a ledger account should be equal to the total value on the credit side of the ledger. In a situation where the sum of the debit side and the credit side of the ledger are not the same, a difference between the two sides should be calculated. This difference is called a closing balance. This is the amount that is posted to the trial balance.

The process of calculating the difference between the two sides (debit and credit sides) of the account, and closing the ledger account is called a balancing-off account. A balancing -off ledger accounts can also be called closing ledger accounts. How the closing balances are presented in the ledger depends on whether the account is related to balance sheet (assets, liabilities and equity) or income statement (income, revenue and expenditure). The closing balance is called balance c/d in the ledger related to balance sheet because the figure will be carried forward to the next accounting period. Closing balance in the ledger related to income statement is called an income statement because it will be transferred to the income statement as income earned or expense incurred for the period.

If the total of the debit entries is greater than the total of the credit entries, then the account is said to have a debit balance. If otherwise, it is called a credit balance. The closing balances on ledgers are posted into trial balance. The debit balances are transferred to the debit side of the trial balance, while the credit balances are posted to the credit side of the trial balance

ILLUSTRATION

Here is an example of a ledger related to a balance sheet.

You are required to balance off the account given below:

Bank Accounts			
	$		$
Bank	5,000	Purchases	850
		Motor Vehicle	1,350
		Rent Expense	900

SOLUTION

Bank Accounts

	$		$
Bank	5,000	Purchases	850
		Motor Vehicle	1,350
		Rent Expense	900
		Balance c/d	1,900
	5,000		5,000
Balance b/d	1,900		

Note: The $1,900 is a debit balance, and it should be transferred to the debit balance of a trial balance.

ILLUSTRATION

Here is an example of a ledger related to an income statement.

Purchases Accounts

2015	$		$
Jan. 15 Bank	12,500		

You are required to balance off the ledger above:

Solution

Purchases Account

2015	$	2015	$
Jan. 15 Bank	12,500	Jan. 31 income statement	12,500

Note: The above account has a debit balance of $12,500, and it should be transferred to the debit side of a trial balance.

ILLUSTRATION 1.8a

Mr. Smith commenced a business on January 1, 2015 with a sum of $50,000 which he paid into his bank account.

He bought the following items and paid by checks immediately:

i.	Jan. 2 Motor vehicle	$10,000
ii.	Jan. 2 Furniture	$5,000
iii.	Jan.15 Goods for resale	$12,200

The following expenditures were also incurred.

i.	Jan.2 Paid transport fare $700
ii.	Jan. 21 Purchase of stationery items for use in the office $200

You are required to balance off the ledger.

SOLUTION

Capital Accounts

2015	$	2015	$
Jan. 31 Balance c/d	50,000	Jan.1 Bank	50,000
		Feb. 1 Balance b/d	50,000

Bank Accounts

2015	$	2015	$
Jan. 1 Capital	50,000	Jan. 2 Motor vehicle	10,000
		Jan. 2 Furniture	5,000
		Jan. 15 Purchases	12,200
		Jan. 2 transport	700
		Jan. 21 Stationery	200

		Jan. 31 Balance c/d	21,900
	50,000		50,000
Feb. 1 Balance b/d	21,900		

Motor Vehicle Account

2015	$	2015	$
Jan. 2 Bank	10,000	Jan. 31 Balance c/d	10,000
Feb. 1 Balance b/d	10,000		

Furniture Account

2015	$	2015	$
Jan. 2 Bank	5,000	Jan. 31 Balance c/d	5,000
Feb. 1 Balance b/d	5,000		

Purchases Account

2015	$	2015	$
Jan. 15 Bank	12,200	Jan. 31 income statement	12,200

Transport Account

2015	$	2015	$
Jan. 2 Bank	700	Jan. 31 income statement	700

Stationery Accounts

2015	$	2015	$
Jan. 21 Bank	200	Jan. 31 income statement	200

1.9   Trial Balance

A trial balance has both debit column and credit column. All the balances in the ledger accounts are transferred to the trial balance. A debit balance in the ledger will be recorded in the debit column of the trial balance, while a credit balance in the ledger will be recorded in the credit column of the trial balance.

A Trial balance can now be defined as a list of account balances drawn up to ascertain the arithmetical accuracy of the posting into the various ledgers. A trial balance is a proof of an arithmetical accuracy of postings to ledgers.

1.9.1 Purposes of a Trial Balance

The following are the purposes of a trial balance:

1. It provides a proof of an arithmetical accuracy of posting into the ledgers.

2. It provides a basis for the preparation of financial statements.

3. It facilitates easy location of errors.

4. It provides a means for determining whether or not the double entry principles have been applied.

ILLUSTRATION 1.9.1a

Extract a simple trial balance from the transactions below for the end of January, 2014:

$

Jan. 1	Started business with bank deposit	25,000
Jan. 2	Bought goods for resale by check	5,000
Jan. 3	Bought motor vehicle by check	2,500
Jan. 4	Sold goods to J. Morgan	1,500
Jan. 5	Bought goods from F. Jane on credit	4,000

SOLUTION

Bank Account

2014	$	2014	$
Jan. 1 Capital	25,000	Jan.2 purchases	5,000
		Jan. 3 Motor vehicle	2,500
		Jan.31 Balance c/d	17,500
	25,000		25,000
Feb.1 Balance b/d	17,500		

Capital Account

2014	$	2014	$
Jan. 31 Balance c/d	25,000	Jan. 1 Bank	25,000
		Feb. 1 Balance b/d	25,000

Purchases Accounts

2014	$	2014	$
Jan. 2 Bank	5,000		

| Jan.5 F. Jane | 4,000 | Jan.31 Income statement | 9,000 |
| | 9,000 | | 9,000 |

Motor Vehicle Account

2014	$	2014	$
Jan. 3 Bank	2,500	Jan. 31 Balance c/d	2,500
Feb. 1 Balance b/d	2,500		

Sales Accounts

2014	$	2014	$
Jan. 31 Income statement	1,500	Jan. 4 J. Morgan	1,500

J. Morgan

2014	$	2014	$
Jan. 4 Sales	1,500	Jan. 31 Balance c/d	1,500
Feb. 1 Balance b/d	1,500		

F. Jane

2014	$	2014	$
Jan. 31 Balance c/d	4,000	Jan. 5 Purchases	4,000
		Feb.1 Balance b/d	4,000

Trial balance as at 31st January, 2014

	$	$
Bank	17,500	
Capital		25,000
Purchases	9,000	
Motor vehicle	2,500	
Sales		1,500
J. Morgan	1,500	
F. Jane		4,000
	30,500	30,500

A long list of information may be provided from which a candidate is required to prepare a trial balance.

The rules to apply are as follows:

1. All assets must have debit balances
2. All expenses must have debit balances
3. All liabilities must have credit balances
4. All provisions must have credit balances
5. All revenues and incomes must have credit balances
6. Capital and accumulated depreciation must have credit balances

Illustration 1.9.1b

Below is a list of balances extracted from the books of Mr. Cowbell on 31st January, 2013. Use the above rules to prepare a trial balance.

	$
	$
Cash at Hand	5,150
Cash at Bank	6,850
Stock(Inventory)	4,500
Debtors(Accounts Receivable)	1,600
Motor Vehicles	5,000

Land and Buildings		10,000
Office Equipment		2,000
Plant & Machinery		3,000
Capital		30,000
Salaries		1,500
Insurance		1,000
Discount Received		200
Returns Outwards		150
Returns Inwards		50
Provision for bad debts(Allowance for doubtful debts)		800
Bills Payable		2,000
Bills Receivable		6,000
Creditors(Accounts Payable)		5,000
Drawings		1,750
Accumulated Depreciation		900
Rent Received		9,350

Solution

Mr. Cowbell

Trial balance as at 31st January, 2013

Date	Description	Dr.	Cr.
2013		$	$
Jan. 31	Cash at Hand	5,150	
Jan. 31	Cash at Bank	6,850	
Jan. 31	Stock(Inventory)	4,500	

Date	Account	Debit	Credit
Jan. 31	Debtors(Account Receivable)	1,600	
Jan. 31	Motor Vehicles	5,000	
Jan. 31	Land & Buildings	10,000	
Jan. 31	Office Equipment	2,000	
Jan. 31	Plant & Machinery	3,000	
Jan. 31	Capital		30,000
Jan. 31	Salaries	1,500	
Jan. 31	Insurance	1,000	
Jan. 31	Discount Received		200
Jan. 31	Returns Outwards		150
Jan. 31	Returns Inwards	50	
Jan. 31	Provision for bad debts		800
Jan. 31	Bills Payable		2,000
Jan. 31	Bills Receivable	6,000	
Jan. 31	Creditors(Accounts Payable)		5,000
Jan. 31	Drawings	1,750	
Jan. 31	Accumulated Depreciation		900
Jan. 31	Rent Received		9,350
		48,400	48,400

NOTE:

A financial statement is prepared from the information contained in the trial balance. If there is any additional information aside from the trial balance, both the information contained in the trial balance and additional information will be used to prepare a financial statement.

Note: If you are given a trial balance, and additional information, and you are asked to prepare a financial statement, you need to apply the rule of double entry to all items in the additional information by treating each transaction twice in the financial statements. Items of a trial balance need not be treated twice during the preparation of financial statements because they have already passed through the rule of double entry during the preparation of ledgers.

1.10 An Introduction to Financial Statements of a Sole Trader

1.10.1 An Introduction to an Income Statement

The main objective of every business entity is to realize a profit. No company intends to make a loss. Earning a continuous profit may not be very easy for an organization because of some reasons. Few of the reasons are mentioned below:

1) Exorbitant and Extravagant spending

2) Unfavorable government policy

3) Low sales

A loss may not be totally avoided in a business entity because of the aforementioned factors.

How can the performance of a business be determined? The answer to this question is found in an income statement which can also be referred to as profit and loss accounts. The income statement is a statement that shows the financial performance of a business entity at a particular period. These periods can be monthly, quarterly and annual.

Profit can be specifically divided into two, namely gross profit and Net profit

Gross Profit

How to determine a gross profit or a gross loss? When sales revenue is greater than the cost of the goods sold, we have a gross profit, but if otherwise, we have a gross loss. The sales revenue is the value at which goods are sold. The cost of goods sold is the total cost involved in putting goods in a saleable condition. Costs such as purchase cost, carriage inward, costs of renovating or repair of the product are regarded as costs of the goods when added together. Trading account is prepared to get gross profit or loss.

Look at the following illustration

Calculate the gross profit or gross loss for the following entities:

Business	Sales	Cost of Sales	Gross profit
X	$15,000	$15,050	($50)
Y	$6,500	$5,600	$900
Z	$10,300	$9,560	$740

Explanations:

The negative value signifies loss while positive values denote profit. It means that company X makes a gross loss of $50 while both companies Y and Z earn gross profits of $900 and $740 respectively.

NET PROFIT

Net Profit found in the income statement (profit and loss accounts) is the gross profit plus other incomes such as commission received, rent received, etc. less other expenses such as salary, rent paid, repair and maintenance of machinery, advertisement, etc. Where the total income is higher than the total expenses, we say there is a Net Profit but if otherwise there is a Net Loss. Profit and Loss account is prepared to determine Net Profit or Net Loss.

In conclusion, the end result of a trading account is a gross profit or a gross loss, while the end result of profit and loss account is a net profit or a net loss. Therefore, the preparation of a trading, profit and loss accounts gives us two sections called gross profit/loss and net profit/loss. The account can also be referred to as an income statement. A statement of comprehensive income has replaced a trading, profit and loss accounts, and a statement of financial position has replaced a balance sheet, according to the new Accounting Standards

ILLUSTRATION 1.10.1a

The trial balance below was extracted from the books of Gagar Ltd.

You are required to prepare Income statement or Statement of Comprehensive Income (Trading, Profit and Loss Accounts) for the year ended December 31, 2013.

	Dr.	Cr.
	$	$
Sales		19,250
Purchases	15,100	
Lighting expenses	950	
Rent received		900
Commission earned		150
Rent paid	1,450	
General expenses	300	
Salaries and wages	1,000	
Fixtures and Fittings	2,500	

Accounts receivable	3,400	
Accounts payable		4,550
Bank	7,550	
Cash	100	
Drawings	3,500	
Capital		11,000
	35,850	35,850

SUGGESTED SOLUTION:

Gagar Ltd.

Income Statement or Statement of Comprehensive income (Trading, Profit and Loss Accounts) for the year ended December 31, 2013.

	$	$
Sales		19,250
Less Purchases		15,100
Gross profit		4,150
Add other income:		
Rent received	900	
Commission	150	
		1,050
Total Income		5,200
Less expenses:		
Lighting expenses	950	
Rent paid	1,450	
General expenses	300	
Salaries & wages	1,000	
		3,700
Net profit		1,500

Note:

We assumed that all the goods purchased were sold. Where all the goods purchased were sold, the cost of goods sold will be equal to purchases.

Where parts of the total goods purchased were not sold, there will be a closing stock normally called inventory. The closing stock should be deducted from the total goods purchased to get the cost of the goods sold for the period.

It can be demonstrated below:

Cost of goods sold = Purchases - Closing Stocks

Purchases in accounting are goods purchased for resale in a normal business of an organization.

Sales are goods sold in a normal business of an organization. Example, if the normal business of ATY enterprise is the selling of school bags, any school bag sold by ATY enterprise is regarded as a part of sales. If a computer is sold by the enterprise, the selling of the computer cannot be called sales but a disposal of an asset because the selling of the computer is not a normal business of ATY enterprise.

Note: Stock is now known as inventory.

1.10.2 An Introduction to Statement of Financial Position

A statement of financial position is a statement that shows the values of assets of the business, liabilities of the business, and funds contributed by the owners of a business entity. According to International Financial Reporting Standards, a balance sheet has been replaced by a statement of financial position.

This study needs to be demystified because of some beginners or those people who do not have previous knowledge of accounting. As a result of this, we will still make use of Balance sheet. Statement of financial position as required by International Financial Reporting Standards will be dealt with in our subsequent studies.

ILLUSTRATION 1

Refer to **Trial Balance of Gagar Ltd. in "illustration 1.10.1a".**
You are required to prepare a balance sheet as at that date.

Suggested Solution:

Gagar Ltd.

Statement of Financial Position (Balance Sheet as at December 31, 2013)

	$	$
Assets		
Fixed Assets:		
Fixtures & Fittings		2,500
Current Assets:		
Cash	100	
Bank	7,550	
Accounts Receivable	3,400	
	11,050	
Less:		
Current Liabilities		
Accounts Payable	4,550	
Working Capital		6,500
		9,000
Capital	11,000	
Net Profit	1,500	
	12,500	
Less Drawings	(3,500)	
		9,000

CHAPTER 2

Assets, Equity and Liabilities

Assets

In an accounting for beginners, an asset can be defined in the following ways:
- An Asset can be defined as an economic resource acquired and owned by an individual or a business entity.
- It can be defined as property, and valuable items belonging to a business entity, such as cash, inventory, machinery that can be used to produce goods or other things, office building from which primary operation of the business is being carried out, and business image that makes people to patronize your business.
- Asset can also be defined as item possessed by a business entity from which future economic benefits are expected to flow to the company.

> According to International Accounting Standard Board; an asset is a resource controlled by an entity as a result of past events and from which future economic benefits are expected to flow to the entity (IASB).

Assets can be classified into Current Assets and Non- Current Assets (Fixed Assets). The distinction between current assets and non - current assets can be based on the length of time in which the future economic benefits from the assets are expected to flow to the business entity. The difference between the current assets and non - current assets can be determined by the period of time in which assets will be used for business activity.

Current Assets are assets that a company is expected to use within one year from the date of reporting.

Non-currents assets are assets from which economic resources are expected to flow to the business for more than a year.

All assets are recorded in the balance sheet. Non-current assets are different from current assets because they are depreciated either monthly or annually. The values of depreciation are treated as depreciation expenses in the **profit and loss accounts** for each year.

Types and Classification of Assets

Assets	Classification	Description
Plant and Machinery	Non-Current	Used for the production of goods and services
Motor Vehicle	Non-Current	Used for the carriage of goods and commuting staff
Computer Equipment	Non-Current	Used for the processing of data and keeping of files
Office Building	Non-Current	It is a place in which daily business activities are being carried out
Inventory	Current	Materials or stocks awaiting sales
Cash	Current	Cash at hand or in the office
Receivables	Current	Money owed by customers

Non-Current Assets can also be subdivided into two. The two types of non-current assets are:
i.   Tangible Fixed Assets
ii.   Intangible Fixed Assets

Tangible Fixed Assets are assets that exist in physical form such as land and buildings, equipment, plant and machinery and long term financial investment. Tangible assets are assets that can be seen and touched.

Intangible Assets are assets that do not exist in physical form. Assets such as Goodwill, patent right, copyrights and trademarks are intangible assets.

EQUITY

Equity is the amount of funds or assets invested by owners of business into the business. It is the net worth of the business. It is the capital that remains after all liabilities have been paid from the assets. It can be demonstrated by an accounting equation.

Assets – Liabilities = Equity

From the equation above, we can say that equity is the net worth of a business entity. According to (IASB), Equity is the residual interest in the assets of a company after deducting all liabilities.

Equity comprises the following:
1. Common stocks or Ordinary Shares
2. Preferred Stocks or Preference Shares (irredeemable)
3. Retained Earnings
4. Revaluation Surplus

Equity may increase or decrease at each particular period based on what happens to any of the components of equity. For example, if any of the components of equity listed above increases, there will be an impact of the increase on equity, and if any of the components of equity decreases, there will be an impact of the decrease on equity.

All equities are posted to balance sheet.

LIABILITIES

From a lay person viewpoint, a liability is an obligation you owed another person. It is an obligation of an individual or a business entity to pay cash or other resources to another party. It is a promise made by an entity to pay back other parties for the use of their assets. One of the most acceptable definitions of a liability is the one used by International Accounting Standards Board (IASB). According to the IASB, a liability is a present obligation of an enterprise arising from past events, the settlement of which is expected to result in an outflow from the enterprise of resources embodying economic benefits.

Liabilities can be classified as current liabilities, and Long-term liabilities (Non- current liabilities) based on their timing differences. The due date of payment for current liability is within a year, while that of Long-term liability is more than a year. All liabilities are posted to balance sheet. The followings are the brief explanations of each item of liabilities

Bank Overdraft: It is an extra amount of money you withdrew from your bank account aside from the original bank balance. It is a current liability.

Short -term Bank Loan: It is the money borrowed by an entity from a bank. It is a current liability.

Accounts Payable: They are the total values of goods sold to you on credit by suppliers. They are current liabilities.

Long –term Bank Loan: It is an amount of money you borrowed from a financial Institution. It is a long-term liability.

Debenture: It is a certificate of agreement of loan issued by the lender to the borrower. It is a long-term liability.

Accrued Wages & Salaries: They are the wages and salaries owed to workers. They are current liabilities.

Accrued Tax: It is the tax owed for the year. It is a current liability.

Unclaimed Dividends: They are the dividends owed to the owners of a company. They are current liabilities.

CHAPTER 3

Accounting Equation

Accounting equation is an appropriate equation that demonstrates the principle of double entry bookkeeping.

Accounting equation can be demonstrated below:

1. Assets = Capital + Liabilities

2. Assets = Owners' equity + Liabilities

3. Assets = Shareholders' Equity + Liabilities

Accounting equation can be represented in any of the above equations. The kind of ownership of a business determines the suitable equation to be used for the business. The equation "1" is a general accounting equation. Equation "2" is meant for a sole proprietorship business while equation "3" is meant for a limited liability company.

What the business owns minus what the business owed will be equal to the capital. The equation which shows what the business owns, what the business owed, and the net worth of the business or owners' equity is called an **accounting equation**.

The following two statements are important if you are setting up a business:

1) You have to contribute personal financial resources for the starting up of the business.

2) You can also obtain funds from external sources.

Where statement "1" alone is applicable, and statement "2" is excluded in setting up a business; we say a business is financed by capital contributed by the owner. This can be demonstrated by: Resources in the business = Resources supplied by the owner

The financial resources contributed by the owner of the business are called capital, while the summation of all financial resources in the business is referred to as Assets.
The accounting equation where a business is financed by capital contributed by the owner is:

Assets = Capital

It means that the whole business is solely financed by the owner of the business.
Where statement "1" and statement two above are applicable together, the accounting equation will change to:

Assets = Capital + Liabilities

Liabilities are the funds provided by the people other than the owner of the business. The owner of the business is indebted to the providers of the finance, and hence he has to pay them back.

From the above, we can conclude that total assets can be divided into the financial resources supplied by the owner of the business and funds contributed by people other than the owner of the business. The two sides of every accounting equation will always be equal to each other no matter how you present it. The equation is the foundation for double entry bookkeeping in accounting.

Example

Mr. Jackson contributed $2,000 on the 2nd of February, 2012 as capital for a new business, placing it with a bank on the same date. He obtained a loan of $800 from a friend on the 3rd of February, 2012. He acquired computer equipment by paying check of $2,600 and he is having a cash balance of $200 in his bank account (bank balance) at the end of the Month. You are required to represent the above information in an accounting equation.

Solution:

$$Assets = Owner's\ Equity + Liabilities$$
Computer equipment + Bank balance = Owner's Equity + Liabilities
$$\$2,600 + \$200 = \$2,000 + \$800$$
$$\$2,800 = \$2,800$$

From the above, total assets are $2,800. The total assets comprise of computer equipment and bank balance. The capital contributed to start the business is owner's equity while the loan he obtained from a friend is recognized as a liability.

If any of the components of the accounting equation above changes, there will be an impact of the change on other components. For example, if owner's equity increases by $100, Assets also will be increased by $100. This is one of the applications of double entry principle. The principle states that for every debit entry, there must be a corresponding credit entry, and for every credit entry there must be a corresponding debit entry.

A statement of financial position is not the first statement to be prepared in accounting, but for the simplicity of our study, we will start with it. We will only bypass the accepted procedures of the recording of financial transactions for easy understanding of accounting equation. Each of these procedures will be discussed in details in our subsequent studies. The procedures we are going to by-pass are as follows:

1. Journal Entries
2. Ledgers Entries
3. Preparation of trial balance

4. Income statement

Lets us now start our illustration with the statement of financial position.

1. Introduction of Capital

On July 1, 2013, Mr. Smith started a business by depositing $80,000 into a bank account specially opened for the business. You are required to prepare a statement of financial position for this transaction.

The effect of this transaction is an increase of bank deposit of $80,000 and an increase of capital contributed by Mr. Smith.

The statement of financial position will be as follows:

Mr. Smith

Statement of financial position as at 1st July, 2013.

$

Asset:

  *Cash at bank   80,000

*Capital   80,000

This is always the way information is presented in the statement of financial position.

2. Acquisition of an asset

On 15th July, 2013, Mr. Smith acquired office premises for $41,000, and paid by check immediately.
Record this transaction in a statement of financial position.

Solution

The effect of this transaction is that cash in the bank will be reduced by $41,000 and non-current asset (office premises) increases by $41,000.

Mr. Smith
Statement of financial Position as at 15th July 2013

	$
Asset:	
*Office premises	41,000
*Cash at bank (80,000 - 41,000)	<u>39,000</u>
	<u>80,000</u>
Capital	**<u>80,000</u>**

3. Purchase of an asset on credit

On 17th July, 2013, Mr. Smith bought goods from D. Dandy for $20,000 and promised to pay him next month. Record this in a statement of financial position.
The effect of this is that assets will increase and liability also will increase.

Mr. Smith
Statement of financial position as at 17th July, 2013

	$
Asset:	

Office premises	41,000
*Inventory	20,000
Cash at bank	39,000
	100,000

Liabilities

*Accounts payable	(20,000)
Net Asset	80,000

Capital	80,000

4. Sales of current asset for immediate payment

On 19th July, 2013, Mr. Smith sold goods which cost $1,500, for cost price to ZP Ltd who paid immediately by check.
Record this transaction in the statement of financial position.

The effect which this transaction will have on the equation is that one asset (cash at bank) will increase while another asset (inventory) will decrease.

Statement of financial position as at 19th July,2013.

	$
Assets:	
Office premises	41,000
*Inventory (20,000- 1,500)	18,500
*Cash at bank (39,000 +1,500)	40,500
	100,000

Liabilities

Accounts payable   (20,000)

                                     80,000

Capital   80,000

5. Sales of a current asset on credit

On the 25th July, 2013, Mr. Smith sold goods which cost $500 to Mrs. Jeff at the same cost price of $500.
How will the transaction appear on the statement of financial position?

The effect of this transaction will be an increase in asset (Accounts receivable) and a decrease in an asset (Inventory)

Statement of financial position as at 25th July,2013

                                       $

Asset:

Office Premises   41,000

*Inventory (18,500 – 500)   18,000

*Accounts receivable   500

Cash at Bank   40,500
                                   100,000

Liabilities:
Accounts payable   (20,000)
                                   80,000

Capital	<u>80,000</u>

6. Collection of a liability

On the 26th July 2013, Mr. Smith received a check worth $400 from Mrs. Jeff for part payment of her debt.

The recording of this transaction is to increase (asset) cash at bank and decrease asset (accounts receivable).

Statement of financial position as at 26th July 2013

	$
Assets:	
Office Premises	41,000
Inventory	18,000
*Accounts receivable (500 – 400)	100
*Cash at bank (40,500 + 400)	<u>40,900</u>
	100,000
Liabilities:	
Accounts payable	<u>(20,000)</u>
	<u>80,000</u>
Capital	<u>80,000</u>

7. Payment of a liability

On the 28th July 2013, Mr. Smith paid a check of $15,000 to D. Dandy for goods purchased from him on credit.

The effect that this transaction will have on the accounting equation is that, Asset (cash at bank) will decrease, and the liability (accounts payable) will decrease.

Statement of Financial Position as at July 30, 2013

	$
Assets:	
Office Premises	41,000
Inventory	18,000
Accounts receivable	100
*Cash at bank (40,900 –15,000)	25,900
	85,000
Liabilities:	
*Accounts payable (20,000 - 15,000)	(5,000)
	80,000
Capital	80,000

CHAPTER 4

THE EFFECT OF PROFIT OR LOSS ON CAPITAL

Profit in an accounting perspective is the amount by which revenue is higher than the sum of all costs incurred to generate the profit. Revenue is the sales value of goods sold. It can also be called an income earned from a service rendered. Revenue from goods sold is the unit price of each commodity multiplied by the number of units sold. There are two major types of profit. They are gross profit and net profit.

Gross profit is the revenue minus the direct cost of goods sold. Net profit is the revenue minus the total direct cost of goods sold, and indirect expenses (overhead) incurred during the time of earning the revenue. To be precise, we can say that net profit is a gross profit minus indirect expenses.

How Does Profit or Loss Affect Capital?

The profit we are talking about here is the net profit. The capital at every beginning of an accounting period is called opening capital. At the end of an accounting period, the capital becomes closing capital.

If a net profit is made during an accounting year, the profit will be added to the opening capital to get the closing capital for the year. The effect of the profit earned during the year is to increase the capital at the end of the year (closing capital). If a net loss is made during the accounting period, the loss will be deducted from the opening capital to get the closing capital. The effect of the loss is to decrease the capital.

The effect can be demonstrated below:

Opening capital + Net Profit = Closing Capital

Opening Capital – Net Loss = Closing Capital

Illustration1

Ajax Ltd., a dealer of home appliances realized revenue of $100,000 on the 5th of January, 2014 from the sales of home appliances during the month. The cost of the goods sold is $69,000. Indirect expenses of $21,000 were incurred to generate the sales in the same month. The company has a capital of $250,000 as at 1st January, 2014. You are required to calculate the capital as at 31st January 2014.

Suggested Solution:

Calculation of Net profit:

	$
Sales	100,000
Less: cost of goods sold	69,000
Gross Profit	31,000
Less: Indirect expenses	21,000
Net Profit	10,000

The Net profit is $10,000.

We can now calculate the capital as at 31st January, 2014 (closing capital).

Opening capital + Net Profit = Closing capital

$250,000 + $10,000   = $260,000

The capital as at 31st January, 2014 is $260,000. We can see that when profit is realized in a period, the capital will be increased by the amount of the profit.

ILLUSTARTION 2

Lets us use the same question in illustration 1, but assume the expenses increased to $36,000. You are required to calculate the capital at the end of the month (as at 31st January, 2014).

Solution:

Step1: Calculate the Net profit or Loss.

	$
Sales	100,000
Less: Cost of Goods Sold	69,000
Gross Profit	31,000
Less: Expenses	36,000
Net loss	(5,000)

Step 2: Determine the capital as at the end of the month.

Opening capital – Net Loss = Closing Capital
$250,000 - $5,000 = $245,000

The capital at the end of the month is $245,000. We can see that the capital decreases from $250,000 to $245,000 because net loss is a negative figure and always reduces the capital.

In conclusion, we can say that Net profit increases capital and Net loss decreases the capital. **As we have earlier discussed**, capital can also be referred to as owners' equity or shareholders' equity.

CHAPTER 5

5. Books of Accounts and Bookkeeping

Bookkeeping is a systematic recording of financial transactions in the books of accounts of a business. It starts from the issuing of source documents and ends in the preparation of a trial balance.

The various stages involved in bookkeeping are:
- Issuing of Source documents
- Recording the source documents to their respective books of original entry.
- Recording the books of original entry to their respective ledgers
- Posting the ledger balances into a trial Balance

5.1 Source Documents

It is important to explain the meaning of a business activity before we proceed with the definition of source documents. A business activity is a financial transaction that occurs during a daily business of an enterprise or a company. It can also be referred to as a financial transaction or a business transaction.

During a daily business activity, an evidence showing authenticity of a financial transaction is generated. The paper proof generated each time a business transaction takes place is called a source document or a business document. In a business transaction, a source document is an evidence that shows that a financial transaction has actually occurred. For example, if a business issues a check to a supplier of computer systems in payment for the supply, and the supplier at the same time issues a receipt acknowledging the collection of the check, the check, and the receipt are source documents.

Source documents are the documents issued each time there is an accounting or a business transaction. It is the only evidence that can be used to prove that a business transaction has actually taken place. Every financial or accounting transaction starts with source documents. The following are the examples of accounting source documents:

5.1.1 SALES INVOICE OR SUPPLIER'S INVOICE

It is a document sent by the seller to the buyer showing an evidence of goods supplied on credit. It shows evidence of **credit sales.** It is used to inform the consumer of the type, number, price, and value of the goods supplied to him or her on credit. It provides a very good evidence of a contract of sales and it can be produced in the court of law for a litigation.

The duplicate of the invoice is retained by the supplier for accounting records. It is used by the supplier to record sales day book. The original copy always goes to the purchaser as earlier mentioned and thus becomes his accounting record and forms the basis of recording his purchases day book.

Specimen of a Sales Invoice

Exhibit 5.1.1

Samotex Ltd

No. 5, Obasa, Oyo Rd., Ib. Nig.

Sales Invoice

Your Sales Order:12/B/120
Invoice No. 221
Date: 7/12/14
To:
Adekunle
No. 10, Adeyemo,
Oluyole,Ib. Nig

	Unit Price $	Qty	Total $
Bags of Wheat	2,000	3	6,000
Bags of Rice	9,000	4	36,000
Bags of Semo	2,500	3	7,500
Total			49,500

Amounts in words: Forty nine thousand and five hundred dollars only.

Customer's Signature	Supplier's Signature
Adekunle	Samotex

5.1.2 DELIVERY NOTE

It is a document acknowledging the delivery of goods, and that the goods are in good condition to the buyer. It is frequently called goods delivery note. Delivery note does not contain prices. It contains quantities of goods only.

Specimen of a Delivery Note

Exhibit 5.1.2

Samotex Ltd
No. 5, Obasa, Oyo Rd., Ib. Nig.

Delivery Note

Delivery Note No. 221
Date: 7/12/14

To:
Adekunle
No. 10, Adeyemo,
Oluyole,Ib. Nig

	Qty
Bags of Wheat	3
Bags of Rice	4
Bags of Semo	3
Total	10

Customer's Signature   Supplier's Signature
Adekunle   Samotex

5.1.3 CREDIT NOTES OR CREDIT MEMO

A credit note is always made out by the supplier of goods when customers returned goods which are unsatisfactory. It can also be used to give an allowance where goods are not actually returned, but are for some reasons not worth the full invoice price as a result of the goods being slightly damaged in transit.

It is called a credit note because the account of the customer will be credited with the amount of allowance to show a reduction in the amount owed.

Credit notes are often printed in red to stop them from being mistaken for invoice.

Assume that Mr. Adekunle returned a bag of wheat to Samotex Ltd, the seller on the 28th December, 2014.

Specimen of a Credit Note

Exhibit 5.1.3

```
Samotex Ltd
No. 5, Obasa, Oyo Rd., Ib. Nig.

                        Credit Note No.: 7/22
Date: 28/12/14


To:
Adekunle
No. 10, Adeyemo,
Oluyole,Ib. Nig

                              Unit
                              Price $    Qty    Total $
        Bag of Wheat          2,000      1      2,000

Amount in words: Two thousand dollars

Customer's Signature        Supplier's Signature
        Adekunle                   Samotex
```

5.1.4 DEBIT NOTES

Goods bought from a seller previously may be returned to the seller if the seller agrees. When this occurs, the customer will issue a document called a debit Note to the seller detailing the description of the goods and the reason for the return. It can also be issued by the seller, especially, when an invoice is made out incorrectly and the value of the transaction is being understated. When this occurs, it is normal to correct the error by sending a debit note to the customer.

Exhibit 5.1.4

```
Samotex Ltd
No. 5, Obasa, Oyo Rd., Ib. Nig.

   Debit Note No.: 8/33
Date: 28/12/14


To:
 P. Smith
No. 10, Aluko,
Oluyole,Ib. Nig

                              Unit
                              Price $    Qty    Total $
        Packet of indomie     2,000       1     2,000

Amount in words: Two thousand dollars

Customer's Signature      Supplier's Signature
      P. Smith                  Samotex
```

SALES RECEIPT

It is used to acknowledge the receipt of money from customers. It is given to customers when customers actually pay for the goods purchased.

VOUCHER

It is an evidential material for the payment of money by a business.

DEPOSIT SLIP

This is a document that serves as an evidence of cash deposited into bank accounts.

WITHDRAWAL SLIP

It is a document used to withdraw cash from a savings account by the owner of the bank accounts.

CHECK

It is used to pay for goods and services. It is used to withdraw money from a current account by the bearer of the check.

COMPUTER GENERATED RECEIPT

It is a document generated from computer showing an evidence of money received from customers.

In conclusion, an evidence is produced each time a business transaction takes place. The paper evidence is called a source document or a business document or an accounting source document. A proof of every business or financial transaction is called a source document. The examples mentioned above are not exhaustive. There are still many more examples of source documents.

5.2. Original Books of Accounts

In order to comply with a systematic recording of a financial transaction, the information extracted from each source document would be transferred to respective books of original entry.

When a business is initially started with few transactions, one or two books of accounts can still be kept for the recording of the business. Where a business is becoming larger, many books of accounts need to be kept for easy and proper accounting.

Books of Original Entry are the books in which all accounting transactions are first recorded. These books show daily description of each business transaction. A respective transaction is entered on each appropriate book. For example, cash is recorded on a cash book. Details of transactions such as names and addresses of buyers are revealed by the books of original entry.

Posting to ledgers are made from each book of original entry.

5.2.1 Types of books of original entry

Books of original entries are referred to as journals or day books. Some frequently used books of original entry are as follows:

1) Sales journal or Sales day book
2) Purchases journal or Purchases day book
3) Returns inwards journal or Returns inwards day book
4) Returns outwards journal or Returns outwards day book
5) Cash book
6) General journal

1. Sales journal is used to record goods sold on credit.
2. Purchases journal is used to record goods purchased on credit.
3. Returns inwards journal is used by a supplier to record goods returned by customers.
4. Returns outwards journal is used to record goods returned to the supplier.
5. Cash book is used to record receipts and payments of cash and check.
6. General journal contains accounting information that cannot be found in other books of original entry. It can also be called journal. General journal is used for the following:
   - The purchase and sale on credit of fixed assets
   - Writing-off bad debts
   - Correction of accounting errors
   - Opening entries. These are the entries needed to open a new set of accounts

- Adjustment for any of the entries in the ledger.

It is necessary to distinguish between trade discounts and cash discounts before we make illustrations of recording to journals or day books.

5.2.2 Trade Discount and Cash Discount

A trade discount is a reduction in a price of a commodity. It is aimed at encouraging patronage. It is commonly allowed on slow moving and expensive goods. A trade discount is a reduction on the catalogue price of an item to enable a retailer to make profit.

Since a trade discount is simply a way of calculating sales, **no entry for trade discount should be made in the double entry records, nor in the sales day book. It is not recorded in the ledger accounts.**

Cash Discount

A cash discount is a reduction in the price of a commodity as a result of prompt payment. It is aimed at encouraging quick payments. It is given by the seller to the buyer. Unlike trade discount, it is posted to a ledger.

5.3 Sales Invoices, Sales Day Book and Ledgers

The information in the sales invoice is posted to sales day book or sales journal. **Sales Invoice** contains only credit sales. All the sales in the sales invoices will be posted to **Sales Day Book** and information in the sales day book will be posted to **sales ledger** and **general ledger**.

Example 5.3

An example of posting credit sales

Note: Assume that the following source documents (sales invoices) are issued by Samotex Ltd. (the seller) to its customers:

Exhibit 5.3a

Samotex Ltd
No. 5, Obasa, Oyo Rd., Ib. Nig.

Sales Invoice

Your Sales Order: 12/B/120
Invoice No. 221

14 December, 2014

To:
Adekunle
No. 10, Adeyemo,
Oluyole,Ib. Nig

	Unit Price $	Qty	Total $
Bags of Wheat	2,000	3	6,000
Bags of Rice	9,000	4	36,000
Bags of Semo	2,500	3	7,500
Total			49,500

Amounts in words: Forty nine thousand and five hundred dollars only

Customer's Signature
Adekunle

Supplier's Signature
Samotex

Exhibit 5.3b

Samotex Ltd
No. 5, Obasa, Oyo Rd., Ib. Nig.

Sales Invoice

Your Sales Order:12/B/121
Invoice No. 222

14 December, 2014

To:
P. Smith
No. 10, Aluko,
Oluyole,Ib. Nig

	Unit Price $	Qty	Total $
Sachets of Spagetti	100	20	2,000
Packets of indomies	2,000	2	4,000
Bags of Semo	2,500	2	5,000
Total			11,000

Amounts in words: Eleven thousand dollars only

Customer's Signature   Supplier's Signature
P.Smith   Samotex

Exhibit 5.3c

Samotex Ltd
No. 5, Obasa, Oyo Rd., Ib. Nig.

Sales Invoice

Your Sales Order:12/B/122
Invoice No. 223
15 December, 2014

To:
Opeyemi
No. 10, Adeyemo,
Oluyole,Ib. Nig

	Unit Price $	Qty	Total $
Bags of Wheat	2,000	3	6,000

Amounts in words: Six thousand dollars only.

Customer's Signature   Supplier's Signature
Opeyemi   Samotex

Exhibit 5.3d

Samotex Ltd
No. 5, Obasa, Oyo Rd., Ib. Nig.

Sales Invoice

Your Sales Order:12/B/122
Invoice No. 224
28 December,2014

To:
R. Robbert
No. 15, Adeyemo,
Oluyole,Ib. Nig

	Unit Price($)	Qty	Total($)
Bags of Wheat	2000	30	60,000
Less 15% trade discount			-9,000
			51,000

Amounts in words: Fifty one thousand dollars only

Customer's Signature	Supplier's Signature
R. Robert	Samotex

SOLUTION:

The accounting information in the sales invoice will be first posted to sales day book.

Note:

Trade discount is a reduction on the catalogue price of an item to enable the retailer to make profit.

Since trade discount is simply a way of calculating sales, **no entry for trade discount should be made in the double entry records, nor in the sales day book. It is not recorded in the ledger accounts.**

Sales day book of Samotex Ltd

Sales Day Book (page 30)

Date	Names	Invoice No.	Folio	Amount
2014				$
Dec. 14	A. Adekunle	221	SL08	49,500
Dec. 14	P. Smith	222	SL10	11,000
Dec. 15	O. Opeyemi	223	SL14	6,000
Dec. 28	R. Robbert	224	SL16	51,000
Transfer to Sales Account			GL124	117,500

Sales Ledger

A. Adekunle (page08)

2014		Folio	$	
Dec.14	Sales	SB30	49,500	

P. Smith (page 10)

2014		Folio	$	

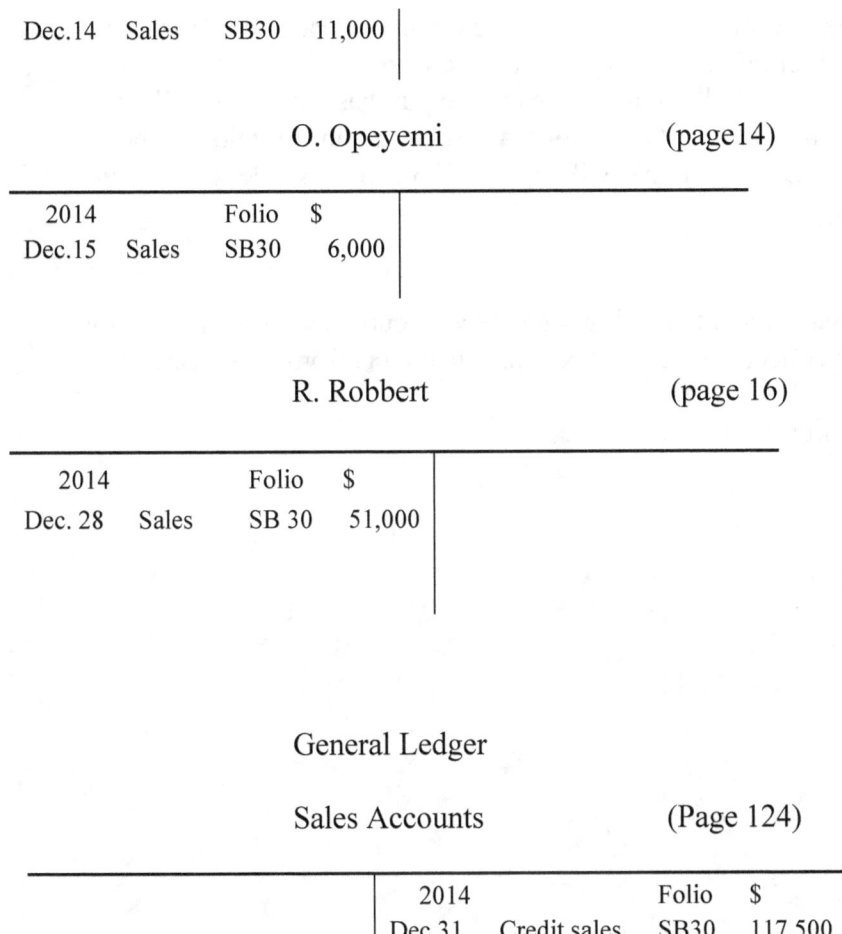

Dec.14   Sales   SB30   11,000

O. Opeyemi   (page14)

2014		Folio	$
Dec.15	Sales	SB30	6,000

R. Robbert   (page 16)

2014		Folio	$
Dec. 28	Sales	SB 30	51,000

General Ledger

Sales Accounts   (Page 124)

	2014		Folio	$
	Dec.31	Credit sales	SB30	117,500
		for the Month		

Note: The credit sales for the month can also be called accounts receivable.

5.4 Purchase Invoices, Purchases Day Book and Ledgers

The information in the purchase invoices is posted to purchases day book or purchases journal. A **purchase Invoice** contains only credit purchases. All the purchases in the purchase invoices will be recorded in the **Purchases Day Book** and information in the purchases day book will be posted to **Purchases ledger** and **general ledger**.

Assume that the following source documents (purchases invoices) are collected by Samotex Ltd. (the buyer) from its suppliers:

Exhibit 5.4a

ASACOM Ltd.

No. 10, Victoria Island, Lagos, Nig.

Purchase Invoice

Your Purchase Order:12/B/120
Invoice No. 333
2 December, 2014

To:
Samotex Ltd.
No. 5, Obasa, Oyo Rd., Ib.
Nig.

	Unit Price $	Qty	Total $
Bags of Wheat	1,000	3	3,000
Bags of Rice	7,000	4	28,000
Bags of Semo	2,000	3	6,000
Total			37,000

Amounts in words: Thirty seven thousand dollars only.

Customer's Signature	Supplier's Signature
Samotex Ltd	ASACOM Ltd.

Exhibit 5.4b

PYZ Ltd
45 Charles Street
Manchester MI 5ZN

Purchase Invoice

Your Purchase Order:12/p/121
Invoice No. 421
December 2, 2014

To:
Samotex
No. 5, Obasa, Oyo Rd. Ib. Nig.

	Unit Price $	Qty	Total $
Sachets of Spagetti	80	30	2,400
Packets of indomies	1,000	4	4,000
Bags of Semo	1,500	8	12,000
Total			18,400

Amounts in words: Eighteen thousand and four hundred dollars only.

Customer's Signature	Supplier's Signature
Samotex	PYZ Ltd

Exhibit 5.4c

ASACOM Ltd.

No. 10, Victoria Island, Lagos, Nig.

Purchase Invoice

Your Purchase Order:12/B/232
Invoice No. 253
6 December, 2014

To:
Samotex
No. 5, Obasa, Oyo Rd. Ib., Nig.
Oluyole,Ib. Nig

	Unit Price ($)	Qty	Total($)
Bags of Wheat	2,000	3	6,000

Amounts in words: Six thousand dollars only.

Customer's Signature	Supplier's Signature
Samotex Ltd	ASACOM Ltd

Exhibit 5.4d

Jasper & Co.
No. 25, Victoria Island, Lagos, Nig
Purchase Invoice

Your purchase Order:13/B/122
Invoice No. 129
9 December, 2014

To:
Samotex Ltd
No. 5, Adeyemo,
Oluyole,Ib. Nig

	Unit Price($)	Qty	Total($)
Bags of Wheat	1000	30	30,000
Less 10% trade discount			-3,000
			27,000

Amounts in words: Twenty seven thousand dollars only.

Customer's Signature	Supplier's Signature
Samotex Ltd.	Jasper & Co.

Purchases day book of Samotex Ltd

	Purchases Day Book			(page 29)
Date	Names	Invoice No.	Folio	Amount
2014				$
Dec.2	ASACOM Ltd.	333	PL18	37,000
Dec. 2	PYZ Ltd.	421	PL19	18,400
Dec. 6	ASACOM Ltd.	253	PL 18	6,000
Dec. 9	Jasper & Co.	129	PL22	27,000
Transfer to Purchases Account			GL122	88,400

Purchases ledger

ASACOMPU Ltd. (Page 18)

2014	$	2014	Folio	$
		Dec. 2 Purchases	PB29	37,000
		Dec. 6 Purchases	PB29	6,000

PYZ Ltd. (Page19)

2014	$	2014	Folio	$
		Dec. 2 Purchases	PB 29	18,400

Jasper & Co. (Page 22)

2014	$	2014	Folio	$
		Dec. 9 Purchases	PB29	27,000

General Ledger

Purchases Accounts (Page 122)

2014	Folio	$	2014	$
Dec. 31 Credit purchases for the year	PB29	88,400		

5.5 Credit Notes, Returns Inwards Day Book and Ledgers

The information in the credit note will be recorded in the return inward day book, and the information in the return inward day book will be transferred to return inward ledger, and general ledger.

Assume that Samotex Ltd. issued the following source documents (credit notes) to its customers that returned some of the goods purchased.

Exhibit 5.5a

Credit Note

Samotex Ltd

No. 5, Obasa, Oyo Rd., Ib. Nig.

Date: 15/12/14

Credit Note No.: 121

To:
A. Adekunle
No. 10, Adeyemo,
Oluyole,Ib. Nig

	Unit Price $	Qty	Total $
Bag of Wheat	2,000	1	2,000

Amount in words: Two thousand dollars only.

Customer's Signature   Supplier's Signature
        A. Adekunle   Samotex

Exhibit 5.5b

Credit Note

Samotex Ltd
No. 5, Obasa, Oyo Rd., Ib. Nig.

Credit Note No.: 122

15 December, 2014

To:
P. Smith
No. 10, Aluko,
Oluyole,Ib. Nig

	Unit Price $	Qty	Total $
Sachets of Spagetti	100	10	1,000

Amounts in words: One thousand dollars only.

Customer's Signature	Supplier's Signature
P. Smith	Samotex

Returns Inwards Day Book   (Page 16)

Date	Names	Credit Note Number	Folio	Amount
2014				$
Dec. 15	A. Adekunle	121	SL 4	2,000
Dec. 15	P. Smith	122	SL 6	1,000
Transfer to sales account			GL124	3,000

Sales Ledger

Dr.   Cr.

A. Adekunle Account   (Page 4)

		Folio	$
2014			
Dec.	Returns		
15	Inward	RI 16	2,000

Dr.   P. Smith Account   (Page 6)   Cr.

		Folio	$
2014			
Dec.	Returns		
15	Inward	RI 16	1,000

General Ledger

Dr.   Returns Inwards Accounts   page (124)   Cr.

		Folio	$	
2014				
Dec. 31	Returns for	RI 16	3,000	
	the month			

5.6. Debit Note, Returns Outwards Day Book and the ledgers

Exhibit 5.6a

ASACOM Ltd.

No. 10, Victoria Island, Lagos, Nig.

Debit Note

Debit Note No. 221

7 December, 2014

To:
Samotex
No. 5, Obasa, Oyo Rd. Ib., Nig.
Oluyole,Ib. Nig

	Unit Price ($)	Qty	Total($)
Bags of Wheat	2,000	1	2,000

Amounts in words: Two thousand dollars only.

Customer's Signature	Supplier's Signature
Samotex Ltd	ASACOM Ltd

Exhibit 5.6b

Jasper & Co.

No. 25, Victoria Island, Lagos, Nig

Debit Note

Debit Note No. 129
December 12, 2014

To:
Samotex Ltd
No. 5, Adeyemo,
Oluyole,Ib. Nig

	Unit Price($)	Qty	Total($)
Bags of Wheat	1000	3	3,000
Less 10% trade discount			-300
			2,700

Amounts in words: Two thousand and seven hundred dollars only.

Customer's Signature	Supplier's Signature
Samotex Ltd.	Jasper & Co.

Returns Outwards Day Book   (page 24)

Date 2014	Names	Debit Note Number	Folio	Amount $
Dec. 7	ASACOMPU	221	PL 6	2,000
Dec. 12	Jasper & Co	129	PL10	2,700

Transfer to sales account   GL12   4,700

Purchases Ledger

ASACOMPU Account   (Page 6)

Date		Folio	$
2014			
	Return		
Dec. 7	outward	RO24	2,000

Jasper & Co   (Page 10)

Date		Folio	$
2014			
	Return		
Dec. 12	outward	RO24	2,700

General ledger
Return Outward Accounts   (Page 12)

Date		Folio	$
2014			
Dec. 31	Return outward for the month	RO24	4,700

CHAPTER 6

Cash Book

6.0. Meaning of a Cash Book

A cash book is a journal in which all cash receipts and payments (including bank deposits and withdrawals are recorded initially, in chronological order, for posting to general ledger. It is established to exercise control over the movement of cash inflow and cash outflow of the business. A cash book balance is regularly reconciled with a bank statement balance as an internal audit measure. As the name suggests, only cash and bank transactions are recorded in the cash book.

A cash book may be referred to as a ledger or a journal (book of original entry). It is normally divided into two parts. The debit side and credit side.

6.0.1. Cash Receipt and payment

Cash collected or received by the business is entered on the debit side while cash paid out of the business is entered on the credit side.

6.0.2. Payment to Bank and Receipt from bank

Check received from a customer by the business and deposited into the bank will be entered on the debited side of a cash book (bank column only). Direct payment to the bank by customers will be debited to a cash book (bank column). Cash deposited into a bank account is debited to the cash book (bank column)

Check issued out and any other payment effected through the bank will be entered on the credit side of the cash book (bank column only). Cash withdrawn from the bank account will be credited to the cash book (bank column).

6.1. Contra Entries

Sometimes cash could be taken from an office to a bank, and cash could be withdrawn from the bank for the office use. When this happens, we have a situation called cross or contra entries. A contra entry is denoted by (c).

Example

Assume that on July 8, a business withdraws $600 from the bank for business use.

You are required to record the above in a cash book.

SOLUTION

Cash Book

Date	Particulars	Folio	Cash	Bank	Date	Particulars	Folio	Cash	Bank
			$	$				$	$
July 8	Bank (c)		600		July 8	Cash (c)			600

Note: The above cash book is an example of two-column cash book.

6.2. Recording into Cash Book

Information in the source documents such as cash receipts, payment voucher, checks received, checks issued, credit card payments etc., are recorded in the cash book.

It has already been explained in the previous chapters of this book that recording in accounting books is based on the rule of double entry principles.

The rule states that for every debit entry there must be a corresponding credit entry and for every credit entry there must be a corresponding debit entry. It means that in a business, an account (ledger) must be open for the receiver, and another account must be open for the giver. As we have learned that cash book can be referred to as a ledger and as well as a book of original entry. In this context, we shall regard cash book as a ledger. It means that all transactions recorded in the cash book will be recorded in another ledger to complete the other leg of a double entry principle. Contra entry will not pass through the rule of a double entry because it has already been recorded twice within the cash book, and as a result of this it shall not be recorded on the other ledger to complete the double entry principles.

6.3. Cash Book and Other Ledgers

Items on the debit side of the cash book will be posted to the credit side of the affected ledger while items on the credit side of the cash book will be posted to the debit side of the concerned ledger. In order to avoid error, cash book should be prepared monthly.

6.4. Types of Cash Book

There are different types of cash book in use today. They are as follows:

1. One-Column Cash Book
2. Two- Column Cash Book
3. Three- Column Cash Book
4. Petty Cash Book

6.4.1. One-Column Cash Book

One-Column Cash Book: This could be a cash account or a bank account controlling cash received or cash paid. It is a cash movement.

It could be cash account containing only cash transactions such as cash received from sales revenue, and income received for services rendered or cash paid for expenses. It could be bank account containing only bank transactions such as check received and check paid. It can also be called a single column cash book.

ILLUSTRATION 1

Enter the transaction below in a cash account of Mr. Jones, and balance off the accounts (close the ledgers) at the end of July 31, 2015.

July 1 cash balance at start $2,000
July 3 bought goods $1,200 in cash
July 5 received $400 from debtors in cash
July 8 paid wages $500 cash
July 10 Cash sales $1,000
July 12 cash drawings $1,300

SOLUTION

Mr. Jones One-column Cash Book (Cash account)

Date		$	Date		$
2015			2015		
July 1	Balance b/f	2,000	July 3	Purchases	1,200
July 5	Debtors	400	July 8	Wages	500
July 10	Sales	1,000	July 12	Drawings	1,300
			July 31	Balance c/d	400
		3,400			3,400
August 1	Balance b/d	400			

ILLUSTRATION 2

The following transactions were extracted from the books of P. James. Enter the transactions in a bank account of Mr. P. James and balance off the accounts at the end of June 30, 2015.

June 1	Debit balance in bank at start $30,000
June 2	Paid into the bank additional cash $10,000
June 3	Bought goods for resale and paid by check $14,000
June 8	Received a check of $16,000 from debtors
June 10	Paid rent $4,000 by check

SOLUTION

P. James Single Column Cash Book (Bank Account)

Date		$	Date		$
2015			2015		
June 1	Balance b/f	30,000	June 3	Purchases	14,000
June 2	Cash	10,000	June 10	Rent	4,000
June 8	Debtors	16,000	June 30	Balance c/d	38,000
		56,000			56,000
July 1	Balance b/d	38,000			

Use of Folio Column

The detail column in an account is the name of the other leg of double entry of the account. It is easy to find the other account of the double entry by mere looking at the detail column provided the books kept are not many. However, when many books are being kept, mentioning the name of the other account may not be sufficient information to find the other half of the double entry (other account) quickly. More information about the location of the other account is needed. This is given by the folio column.

A folio column is added to each account and each book at their extreme right corner for easy reference of the other account or book. In the column, the name of the other book and the number of the page in the other book where the other part of the double entry is recorded will be stated against each and every entry.

In order to ensure that the double entry is complete, the folio column should only be filled in when the double entry has been completed.

Example

An entry for payment of cash into T. Jones' account whose account was on page 12 of the purchase ledger, and the cash recorded on page 29 of the cash book, would have the following folio column entries:

In the cash book; the folio column entry would be PL 12

In the Purchases Ledger; the folio column entry would be CB29

Where:
PL = Purchases Ledger
CB= cash Book

6.4.2. Two-Column Cash Book

Two-column cash book has both cash and bank columns together on either side of a ledger account. All the cash transactions will be recorded under cash column while all bank transactions will be recorded under bank column. At the end of the period, there will be cash and bank balances.

ILLUSTRATION

The following transactions were extracted from the source documents of Jane enterprises, within the month of July, 2015. Record the transactions in the two-column cash book of Jane enterprises and balance off the account as on July 31, 2015.

July 1	Started business with $1,000 cash
July 2	paid wages of $400 in cash
July 3	bought goods $500 by check
July 8	withdrew $600 for business use
July 10	cash sales $800 paid direct into bank
July 12	bought goods for $650 on credit

SOLUTION

Jane Two-Column Cash Book   Page 88

Date	Particulars	Folio	Cash	Bank	Date	Particulars	Folio	Cash	Bank
2015 July			$	$	2015 July			$	$
	Capital	PrL10	1,000						
8	Bank (c)		600		2	Wages	GL28	400	
10	Sales	GL32		800	3	Purchases	PL 30		500
					8	Cash (c)			600
	Balance c/d			300	31	Balance c/d		1,200	
			1,600	1,100				1,600	1,100
Aug.1	Balance b/d		1,200		Aug.1	Balance b/d			300

Note:
PrL = Private Ledger
GL = General Ledger
PL = Purchases Ledger

Cash Discounts

Cash Discount is the amount of reduction in the price of goods sold to a customer as a result of prompt payment. It is an allowance given to a customer for quick payment. It is used to encourage prompt payment.

It can be stated in an absolute value or in a percentage. If it is stated in percentage, the (rate) percentage will be used to multiply the sales value of the goods; the result obtained is the cash discount. Cash discount can either be paid by cash or check.

A business may have two types of cash discounts in its books. They are:

1) Discount received: This is a cash discount received by a business from its suppliers when it pays what it owes them promptly.

2) Discount allowed: This is a cash discount given by a business to its customers when they pay their accounts quickly.

6.4.3 Three -Column Cash Book

It is important to avoid too many entries in the general ledger. As a result of this, two columns for cash discounts are included in the cash book. There is a column for discount allowed on the debit side and discount received on the credit side of the cash book. Only total of each of the column would be recorded in the ledger.

Why is a discount allowed debited, and a discount received credited?

The reasons are as follows:

1) Discount allowed is an expense, and every item that increases expense should be debited in the book of accounts
2) Discount received is an income, and every item that increases income should be credited in the book of account

Examples

The following examples demonstrate the effects of cash discounts in books of accounts of our business:

Example 1

P. James owed us $200. He pays us in cash on May 1, 2014 which is within the time limit applicable for a 10 per cent cash discount. He pays $200 - $20 = $180 in full settlement of his account.

	Effect	Action
1.	Cash entry	
a.	Asset (cash) is increased by $180.	Debit cash account(record $180 to the debit column of Cash book)
b.	Asset (account receivable) is decreased by $180	Credit P. Jones $180
2.	Discount allowed	
a.	Expense (Discount allowed) is increased by $20	Debit Discount allowed account $20
b.	Asset (account receivable) is decreased by $20. $20 being discount allowed to P. Jones.	Credit P. Jones account $20.

Example 2

The business owed S. Steven $9,000. We pay him by check on May 5, 2014 which is within the time limit laid down by him for 2 1/2 percent cash discount. The business will pay $9,000 - $225 = $8,775 in full settlement of the account.

	Effect	**Action**
1.	Check	
a.	Asset (bank) is reduced by $8,775.	Credit bank (record $8,775 to the credit side of bank column)
b.	Liability (account payable) is reduced by $8,775	Debit S. Steven account $8,775
2.	Discount Received	
a.	Income (Discount received) is increased by $225	Credit Discount received account $225
b.	Liability (account payable) is decreased by $225. $225 being discount received from S. Steven	Debit account payable account (S. Steven account $225)

Our Business Cash Book   (Page 52)
Three -Column Cash Book

Date	Particulars	Folio	Disc	Cash	Bank	Date	Particulars	Folio	Disc	Cash	Bank
2014			$	$	$	2014			$	$	$
May						May					
1	P. James	SL30	20	180		5	S. Steven	PL26	225		8,775

General Ledgers

Dr.   Cr.

Discount Allowed Account   (General Ledger 15)

Date		Folio	$	Date		Folio	$
2014				2014			
May 1	P. James	CB52	20				

Dr.   Cr.

Discount Received Account   (General Ledger 16)

Date		Folio	$	Date		Folio	$
2014				2014			
				May 5	S. Steven	CB52	225

Sales Ledger

P. James   Account   (Sales Ledger 30)

Date		Folio	$	Date		Folio	$
2014				2014			
May 1	Balance	b/f	200	May 1	Cash	CB52	180
				May 1	Discount	CB52	20
			200				200

Purchases Ledger

S. Steven Accounts   Purchases Ledger 26

Date		Folio	$	Date		Folio	$
2014				2014			
May 5	Discount	CB52	225	May 1	Balance	b/f	9,000
May 5	Bank	CB52	8,775				
			9,000				9,000

ILLUSTRATION

The following were extracted from the books of Steven Enterprises:

2013	$
March 1	
Cash balance	58
Bank balance	1,308
Accounts receivable accounts:	
B. Popson	240
N. Smith	560
D. Jasper	80
Account Payable:	
U. Adams	120
A. Alice	880
R. Barrack	200

March 2 B. Popson pays us by check, having deducted 2 1/2 percent cash discount ($6); $234.

March 8, we paid R. Barrack his account by check deducting 5 percent cash discount ($10); $190.

March 11, we withdrew $200 cash from the bank for business use; $200.

March 16. N. Smith pays us his account by check deducting 2 1/2 percent cash discount ($14); $546.

March 25, we paid office expenses in cash; $184

March 28, D. Jasper pays us in cash after having deducted 5 percent cash discount ($4); $76

March 29, we paid U. Adams by check less 5 percent cash discount ($6) ; 114

March 30, we pay A. Alice by check less 2 1/2 percent cash discount ($22); $858

SUGGESTED SOLUTION

Our Business

Three-Column Cash Book

Date	Particulars	Folio	Disc.	Cash	Bank	Date	Particulars	Folio	Disc.	Cash	Bank
2013			$	$	$	2013			$	$	$
Mar.						Mar.					
1	Balance	b/f		58	1,308	8	R. Barrack	PL25	10		190
2	B.Popson	SL20	6		234	11	Cash	(c)			200
11	Bank	(c)		200		25	office exp.	GL55		184	
16	N. Smith	SL22	14		546	29	U. Adams	PL29	6		114
28	D. Jasper	SL25	4	76		30	A. Alice	PL31	22		858
						31	Balance	c/d		150	726
			24	334	2,088				38	334	2,088
Apr.											
1	Balance	b/d		150	726						

Sales ledger

B. Popson   (Sales ledger page 20)

Date		Folio	$	Date		Folio	$
2013				2013			
Mar.1	Balance	b/f	240	Mar. 2	Bank	CB11	234
				Mar. 2	Discount	CB11	6
			240				240

N. Smith   (Sales ledger page 22)

Date		Folio	$	Date		Folio	$
2013				2013			
Mar.1	Balance	b/f	560	Mar. 16	Bank	CB11	546
				Mar. 16	Discount	CB11	14
			560				560

A. Jasper Account (Sales ledger page 25)

Date		Folio	$	Date		Folio	$
2013				2013			
Mar.1	Balance	b/f	80	Mar. 28	Cash	CB11	76
				Mar. 28	Discount	CB11	4
			80				80

Purchases Ledger

R. Barrack   (Purchases ledger page 25)

Date		Folio	$	Date		Folio	$
2013				2013			
Mar. 8	Bank	CB11	190	Mar.1	Balance	b/f	200
Mar. 8	Discount	CB11	10				
			200				200

U. Adams   (Purchases Ledger 29)

Date		Folio	$	Date		Folio	$
2013				2013			
Mar. 29	Bank	CB11	114	Mar. 1	Balance	b/f	120
Mar. 29	Discount	CB11	6				
			120				120

A. Alice   (Purchases Ledger page 31)

Date		Folio	$	Date		Folio	$
2013				2013			
Mar. 30	Bank	CB11	858	Mar.1	Balance	b/f	880
May. 30	Discount	CB11	22				
			880				880

General Ledger

Office Expenses   (General Ledger page 66)

Date		Folio	$	Date	Folio	$
2013				2013		
Mar. 25	Cash	CB11	184			

Discount Allowed (General Ledger page 66)

Date		Folio	$	Date	Folio	$
2013				2013		
Mar. 31	Total for the Month	CB11	24			

Discount Received (General Ledger Page 70)

Date	Folio	$	Date		Folio	$
2013			2013			
			Mar. 31	Total for the Month	CB11	38

Bank Overdrafts

The balance in the bank account is often a debit balance. There are some exceptional situations where a company can borrow money from bank by a way of bank overdrafts. This means that a company may withdraw or pay more than its bank balance (the money it has in the bank account). When there are bank overdrafts, the bank balance will no longer be a debit balance but a credit balance.

6.4.4 Petty Cash Book

Any small amount of money held by a responsible officer for meeting duly authorized small expenses, is called a petty cash. The method of keeping petty cash is called imprest system.

When an imprest system is in operation with the petty cash book, a float is established to meet the petty cash payments. At the end of the month, the total amount spent is reimbursed. At any given time, the amount on the paid vouchers and the cash in the hand of the petty cashier should be equal to the amount of the float.

Multiple choice questions

Double Entry Bookkeeping /Accounting Equation

1. Which of the following is wrongly classified?

    A. Warehouse, account receivable, and loan to B. Black
    B. Mortgage of office building, inventory, and computers
    C. Warehouse, Machinery and Loan to B. Black
    D. Loan from bank, account payable and bank overdraft

2. C. Palic is setting up a business. $5,000 is deposited into his bank account. Out of this amount, $650 is borrowed from friends while the remaining balance is his personal money. Calculate the total asset.

    A. $4,450
    B. $650
    C. $5,000
    D. $4,350

3. Mr. Stone started business with $1,900 on February 1, 2012. He made a net loss of $60 at the end of the year. How much is his capital at the beginning of the year 2013?
    A. $1,900
    B. $1,840
    C. $1,960
    D. $2,060

4. Miss Eunice started a business with $2,500 on January, 2010. She earned a net profit of $1,019 at the end of the year, 2010. How much will her capital be at January 1, 2011?
    A. $1,019
    B. $1,901
    C. $2,500
    D. $3,519

5. A payment of an expense---------- assets

A. devalues
B. increases
C. reduces
D. change

6. Payment of accounts payable --------

A. increases assets and reduces liabilities
B. increase assets and increases liabilities
C. decreases assets and decreases liabilities
D. decrease liability and equate asset

7. What effect will an increase in capital have on assets?

A. increase assets
B. decrease assets
C. no effect
D. equate asset

8. The basic accounting equation is -----

A. capital + asset = liability
B. capital = liability + asset
C. capital = liability + asset
D. asset = capital + liability

9. Capital decreases if -------- decreases

A. Revenue
B. Expense
C. Liability
D. Drawings

10. Accounting equation can be best related to-------

A. income
B. assets
C. principles of double entry book-keeping

D. nominal accounts

11. A business has the following items in it.

Building?
Cash $15,000
Plant & Machinery $300,000
Debtors $60,000
Owner's equity $500,000
Loan $250,000
Creditors $25,000

What is the value of the building?

    A. $500,000
    B. $775,0000
    C. $400,000
    D. $450,000

12. Which of the following is not a current asset?

    A. Inventory
    B. Short- term investment
    C. Cash at bank
    D. Bank overdraft

13. Which of the following is not an asset?

    A. Cash
    B. Cash at bank
    C. Account receivable
    D. Tax owed

14. A business has the following items in it.
Mortgage loan $40,000
Account payable $15,000
Account receivable $20,000
Machinery $200,000
Land and Building $520,000

Owner's equity?

What is the value of owner's equity?

A. $658,000
B. $688,000
C. $685,000
D. $720,000

15. A business entity has the following in it

Capital $65,000
Asset ?
Liability $15,000

What is the value of Asset?

A. $70,000
B. $65,000
C. $90,000
D. $80,000

16. An investment of additional cash into a business enterprise results in a/an

A. Increase in asset and increase in capital
B. Decrease in capital and increase in cash
C. Decrease in capital and increase in loan
D. Increase in capital and decrease in cash

17. One of the following stands as a separate item in the basic accounting equation.

A. Owners equity
B. Asset
C. Account receivable
D. Liability

18. Owner's equity has what type of balance?

A. Debit balance
B. Credit balance
C. Negative balance
D. Positive balance

19. Which of the following is an expanded accounting equation for a sole proprietorship?
   A. Assets = Capital + Liabilities
   B. Assets = Owner's capital+ Liabilities
   C. Assets = Liabilities + Owner's equity+ Revenue – Expenses – Owner's drawings
   D. Capital = Asset + Liability – Drawings

20. A change in any item of a basic accounting equation will have effect on how many items?
   A. Only three
   B. At least one
   C. Non of the items
   D. Four

21. Outstanding rent of $600 is paid by the proprietor. The effect on the balance sheet is ------
   A. Both asset and liability remain unchanged
   B. Liability is increased while the asset remain unchanged
   C. Capital Increased while liability decreased
   D. Liability increased while the asset decreased

22. Which of the following will be posted to the proprietor's capital accounts?
   A. Anticipated profit   B. Gross profit   C. Net profit   D. Net sales

23. Steven's capital at January 1, 1999 and December 31, 1999 were $80,000 and $110,000 respectively.
During the year he introduced additional capital of $13,500 and withdrew $8,500 for private use. What is his profit for the year ended January 31, 1999?
   A. $25,000   B.$30,000   C.$96,500   D. $93,500

24. The financial position of an enterprise at a particular time can be ascertained from
    A. Statement of cash flow
    B. Balance sheet
    C. Profit and loss accounts
    D. income statement

25. When a transaction causes an asset account to increase, there is an increase of equal amount in capital or
    A. a decrease of equal amount in the owner's equity account
    B. an increase of equal amount in a liability account
    C. an increase of equal amount in another asset account
    D. a decrease of equal amount in a liability account.

26. To realize an asset means to
    A. use it as collateral
    B. to turn it to cash
    C. to remove it from the company
    D. to evaluate it

27. Which of the following cannot be realized?
    A. machinery   B. debtors   C. Goodwill   D. creditors

28. The golden rule of double entry principles states that----------

A. Debit and credit entry must be recorded and vice versa
B. For every debit entry there must be a corresponding credit entry, and for every credit entry there must be a corresponding debit entry.
C. Debit entry must be recorded before credit entry
D. Assets = Liabilities + Owner's equity

29. Double entry system is ------------

A. A reporting system
B. An accounting system
C. A recording system

D. Credit and debit entry system

30. How do you record cash invested in business by an entrepreneur, in a book of accounts
    B. Debit investment account and credit cash account
    C. Debit cash account and credit investment account
    D. Debit cash account and credit capital account
    E. Debit owner's equity and debit investment account

31. A proof of arithmetical accuracy of various posting in the ledger is a-------------

    A. Financial statement
    B. Balance sheet
    C. Control account
    D. Trial balance

32. If opening capital is $60,000 and closing capital is $58,500. What is the Net Profit or Loss?
    A. Net profit $2,500
    B. Net profit $1,500
    C. Net loss $ 5,5500
    D. Net loss $ 1,500

33. The concept of double entry book-keeping states that
    A. First party receives and the second party gives
    B. For every seller there is a buyer
    C. every debit entry must have a corresponding credit entry, and every credit entry must have a corresponding debit entry.
    D. Every transaction has double entry

34. Which of the following is odd?
    A. Bank overdraft B. Machinery C. Preliminary expenses D. Goodwill

35. Which of the following is a fictitious asset?
    A. Land and Building B. Plant and Machinery C. Preliminary expense D. Prepayment

36. Income received in advance is recorded in the balance sheet
as a/an
A. Intangible Asset B. Goodwill C. Tangible Asset D.
Current liability

37. The excess of current assets over current liabilities is
A. Owners' equity B. Shareholders' funds C. a working
capital D. Net Account payable is

38. When closing stock is overstated, it would increase
A. Gross profit and reduce purchases
B. Gross profit and reduces cost of sales
C. Sales and reduces and increases purchases
D. Purchases and reduce cost of sales

39. Which of the following will be excluded from the calculation
of working capital?
A. Inventory B. overdraft C. prepayment D. Furniture

40. Who invented double entry bookkeeping?
A. Roberto Pacioli B. Sabalele Rio   C. Steven Steigal   D. Luca
Pacioli

Solution to multiple choice questions

1) The correct answer is B. Mortgage of office building, inventory and computers.

Mortgage of office building is a liability and cannot be classified as an asset.
Inventory is an asset and cannot be classified as a liability.
Computers are assets and cannot be classified as liabilities.

2) The correct answer is C. $5,000.
This question can be solved using accounting equation. The equation is:

Asset = Capital + Liability
$5,000 = $4,350 +$650

It can be seen from the above that out of the cash deposited to bank, $4,350 belongs to C. Palic and $650 was borrowed from friends. If these two values are added together, we will get the total asset which is $5,000.

3) The correct answer is B. $1,840.
The capital at the beginning of year 2013 will be:
Capital at February 1, 2012 – Net loss
= $1,900 – $60
= $1,840
Note: Net loss is always deducted from the opening capital to get the closing capital because net loss has a negative value.

4) The correct answer is D) $3,519
The capital at January 1, 2011 =

=January 1, 2010 + Net loss
= $2,500 + $1,019
= $ 3,519

Note: Net profit is always added to opening capital because it is a positive figure.

5) The correct answer is C).
Payment of expenses will definitely reduce assets. You can either pay by cash or bank. Bank and cash are assets from which expenses could be paid from. Either of these two will be reduced whenever there is a payment.

6) The right answer is C) decreases assets and decreases liabilities.
Payment of accounts payable will reduce asset. It will also reduce liability because accounts payable is a liability and once is paid for, it reduces.

Look at the accounting equation here:

Asset = Capital + Liability

The asset reduces by the amount paid from asset (cash or bank) and liability also reduces by the amount of the liability (accounts payable) that was paid.

7) The correct answer is A)
The solution can also be picked from the above equation. If capital increases, assets must also increase. This will be more explained in double entry principles of accounts.

8) The correct answer is D)
Asset = Capital + Liability

9) The correct answer is A)

10) The correct answer is C) principles of double entry book-keeping

11) This question can be solved by a basic accounting equation

ASSETS	$
Building	?
Cash	15,000
Plant and Machinery	300,000
Debtors	60,000

LIABILITIES	$
Loan	250,000
Creditors	25,000
	275000

$$ASSETS = CAPITAL + LIABILITY$$

Building + $375,000 = $500,000 + $275,000
Building + $375,000 = $775,000
Building = $775,000 - $375,000
= $400,000

The correct answer is C) $400,000

12) The correct answer is D) Bank overdraft

13) The correct answer is D) Tax owed
14) The correct answer is C) $685,000
The accounting equation can be used to solve this question.
Assets = Capital +Liabilities

Owner's Equity = Assets – Liabilities

Assets	$
Account receivable	20,000

Machinery	200,000
Land and building	520,000
	740,000

Liabilities	$
Mortgage loan	40,000
Account payable	15,000
	55,000

Owner's Equity = $740,000 – $55,000
$$= \$685,000$$

15) The answer is D) $80,000
The basic accounting equation can be used to solve this equation.

Assets = Capital + Liabilities
Assets = $65,000 +$15,000
$$= \$ 80,000$$

16) A) Increase in asset and increase in capital
17) B) Asset
18) B) credit balance
19) The answer is C)
    Assets = Liabilities + Owner's equity+ Revenue – Expenses – Owner's drawings

20. B	26. B	32. D	38. B
21. C	27. D	33. C	39. D
22. C	28. B	34. A	40. D
23. A	29. C	35. C	
24. B	30. C	36. D	
25. B	31. D	37. C	

REFERENCES:

Frank Wood (12th edition) Business Accounting

Adelaje, T.O. (2015) Basic Financial Accounting (MCQ & A). USA, Createspace

www.accountinghour.com

www.ingramcontent.com/pod-product-compliance
Lightning Source LLC
Chambersburg PA
CBHW072254200526
45168CB00016B/1950